Banners
for All Seasons

How to make creative banners
for holy days and holidays

Joyce Pike
and Anne Robinson

MERIWETHER PUBLISHING LTD.
Colorado Springs, Colorado

M000159441

Meriwether Publishing Ltd., Publisher
PO Box 7710
Colorado Springs, CO 80933-7710

Editors: Rhonda Wray and Sue Trinko
Cover and book design: Janice Melvin
Typesetting: Sue Trinko
Interior illustrations and photography: Joyce Pike and Anne Robinson

© Copyright MMI Meriwether Publishing Ltd.
Printed in the United States of America
First Edition

All rights reserved. No part of this publication, except where specifically noted, may be reproduced, stored in a retrieval system, or transmitted in any form or by any means, electronic, mechanical, photocopying, recording, or otherwise, without permission of the publishers. Permission to reproduce copies of the banner patterns included in this text is granted with the purchase of this book. Copies of these banner patterns are for the use of the purchaser and the purchaser's organization only. They may not be sold or transferred to any third party.

Scripture taken from the HOLY BIBLE, NEW INTERNATIONAL VERSION ®. NIV®. Copyright © 1973, 1978, 1984 by International Bible Society. Used by permission of Zondervan Publishing House. All rights reserved.

Library of Congress Cataloging-in-Publication Data

Pike, Joyce, 1942-
    Banners for all seasons : how to make creative banners for holy days & holidays / Joyce Pike & Anne Robinson.-- 1st ed.
        p. cm.
    ISBN 1-56608-059-2 (pbk.)
        1. Church pennants. I. Robinson, Anne, 1948- II. Title.

BV168.F5 P55 2001
246'.55--dc21

                                                                        2001041034

            2   3   4   5   03   04   05

Dedication

*Dedicated to Him who set us free
To be creative for His glory.*

Contents

Introduction

Let's Celebrate

"Every skilled woman spun with her hands and brought what she had spun..." (Exodus 35:25).

We believe God is stirring his people to restore the visual arts to their rightful place in his church. Dance, film, drama and painting are increasingly coming under his influence, and the ministry of banner-making is just one aspect. Our desire in this book is to present a variety of banners to be used in our churches and other places where Christian seasons and festivals are celebrated.

Always our hope is to create a banner that will glorify God and at the same time visually stimulate a closer encounter with him. As people recreated in Jesus, have we not too long neglected God's creative resources within our beings? Perhaps this is the season for you to draw on the abundance of his gifts and your learned skills to contribute to this visual restoration within his people.

Developing skills takes time and practice, as does slowing the pace of our lifestyles, to allow ourselves to be open to God's inspiration and direction.

Exodus 31:1-6 — "Then the Lord said to Moses, 'See, I have chosen Bezalel son of Uri, the son of Hur, of the tribe of Judah, and I have filled him with the Spirit of God, with skill, ability and knowledge in all kinds of crafts — to make artistic designs for work in gold, silver and bronze, to cut and set stones, to work in wood, and to engage in all kinds of craftsmanship. Moreover, I have appointed Oholiab son of Ahisamach, of the tribe of Dan, to help him. Also I have given skill to all the craftsmen to make everything I have commanded you.'"

As God gave his Spirit, inspiration and skills to the Israeli craftsmen, so too will he fill, inspire and equip us to do his creative will today.

Consider: "All who are skilled among you are to come and make everything the Lord has commanded" (Exodus 35:10).

Foreword

The psalmist, in Psalm 115:2-7, rather scornfully refers to the gods of the nations as being lifeless idols that can neither speak nor see nor hear nor feel. This is in contrast to the God of the people of Israel, whom the psalmist says "does whatever it pleases him" and who certainly speaks, sees, hears and feels. And so our experience as Christians bears testimony to what the psalmist has written, because we know that our God is indeed alive and that he communicates with us in countless ways. He has, of course, communicated to us supremely in the person of our Lord Jesus Christ and also through his Word to us in Holy Scripture. But God also communicates to us in so many other ways, and it is wise for us to be alert, sensitive and open to his communication.

I have found over the years that God has not only spoken to me through the "gentle whisper," as he did to Elijah (1 Kings 19:12), but also through visual images and movement. Banners in a church building or in a Christian celebration do not merely add to the beauty of the place or to the occasion, but they add another dimension through which God speaks to me and makes himself known. I believe that we in the church should be encouraging one another to use our God-given gifts and abilities to create banners, stained glass windows, flower arrangements and other visual images. God can use them to speak to his people and indeed to his world.

I have been greatly encouraged in my Christian pilgrimage by Anne and Joyce. They have allowed themselves to be used by God to create banners that are at once beautiful and worshipful. God speaks to me (and many others) through their banner designs, communicating something of his glory and his presence.

I trust that as God filled Bezalel (Exodus 31:2-3) by his Spirit "with skill, ability and knowledge in all kinds of crafts to make artistic designs …" the people of God in our day will be open to receive the same gifts from him and to use them to create banners and other artistic expressions to glorify God and provide another means by which he may speak to his people.

My hope and prayer is that Anne and Joyce's book will be of help to you in your ministry as one of the Bezalels of today.

Bishop Eric Pike
Farne, Fish Hoek, South Africa

Basic Technique

A Guide on How to Assemble Your Banner

As I have taught banner-making at many workshops over the past years, I have had to devise a technique that was easy, quick and stable. Many of the people I have taught have had limited sewing skills or artistic ability, yet by following the basic steps, they produced beautiful works, worthy of honoring our Creator.

1. Step one is to pray, as it is the Holy Spirit who empowers us to accomplish the work he sets before us.

2. Select the banner design you would like to make. The instructions for each of the banners in this book indicate a specific size consistent with the required construction materials. You may make any one of these banners larger or smaller than the finished dimensions given in the pattern instructions. It will depend on where you want to hang your work.

   To enlarge the graph patterns provided on these pages, use an overhead projector to project the image onto a wall in whatever size you select, and then trace the design onto paper. This projection method of enlargement affords maximum flexibility without proportional measurements.

   To project the image, you will need to make a transparency or use an opaque projector. If neither of these options is available, you can simply photograph the graph pattern with slide film that can be used in any home projector.

   You can also create transparencies of the patterns using your home computer. Simply use a scanner to scan the patterns onto your desktop. Then print the patterns onto transparency film with your printer. Transparency film can be found at most office supply stores.

   The basic design may also be altered at this stage. Just make sure that the message of the banner remains clear.

If you want to change the colors, make a photocopy of the graph pattern in the book and color it in using either pencils or paints. We would encourage you to use your own color sense and make use of the materials you have available in your scrap box. Reproducing someone else's design can become uninspiring if you do not explore your own creativity.

3. Select materials and judge whether you will have enough fabric for each color. Use your full-size template to estimate. (Yardages given are for the dimensions we made each banner and are for 60-inch-wide fabric unless otherwise noted.) Including a variety of textures always ensures variation and adds interest to the finished work.

4. Cut a backing fabric just larger than the design. Muslin or another strong white cotton is usually sufficient to carry the weight of the banner.

5. Lay the paper template flat and place a piece of iron-on interfacing on top (shiny side up), covering the whole of your design. Draw the outline onto the interfacing with a soft-nibbed felt pen. Cut out each piece.

6. Iron each piece of interfacing to the wrong side of the selected fabric and trim. Assemble the pieces on the backing fabric to form your design.

7. Glue and/or sew the pieces into position. A good-quality fabric glue (or glue-gun application) is best to accomplish a neat finish.

8. At this point, it is helpful to view your design from a distance. Check if your color combinations and textures work together and are aesthetically pleasing.

9. Once satisfied, add the finishing touches. Sequins, braids and ribbons are ideal. It is very important to build up a focal point. Applying the trim using fabric glue or a glue gun is far easier and less time consuming than sewing them down.

If your banners are to travel frequently and are to be used in processions outdoors, keep "glued" accessories to a minimum. Sew on all trims and accessories for durability in folding and general wear and tear.

10. Once again hold the banner upright and view from a distance. Make sure the message of the banner is clear and that the focal point is eye-catching. Enjoy assembling your banner, as it affords you the opportunity to stamp your individuality on the design.

11. Finally, attach the banner to the backing cloth, which will be slightly larger than the finished size. As mentioned in step four, a firm muslin is ideal. Tuck in the edges to neaten their appearance and glue down or sew in the conventional manner. Leave openings at the top of the banner for a dowel or attach hanging loops. Once again, view from afar to see if any finishing touches are required, e.g., painting the dowel, attaching tassels to the corners or hanging ribbons down the sides.

Banners are seldom scrutinized close up or inspected for minor assembly errors. It is far more important to let your creative spirit flow and enjoy the work rather than to spend hours trying to perfect it.

In creating this book, we decided to use as many fabric techniques as possible and to integrate them into our designs, thus hoping to add interest to the subjects and to inspire you. Each technique will be discussed briefly in the banner design in which it appears.

The Banners

"The people living in darkness have seen a great light."
— Matthew 4:16

Advent

To emphasize the division between the darkness and God's great light, this banner is comprised of two completely separate sections hanging on a double curtain track. If it is not possible for such a system to work in your church, the back section could be attached to the wall, with the front section hanging on a rod a few inches away from the wall. The photographed banner measures 44 inches by 52 inches and the required fabrics listed below are for that size. The deep blue fabric gives the impression of darkness, with the silver trimming depicting a sharp outline where light and dark meet. All the figures are black with layers of black and white net added to show variation in those who are nearer the light. The quantity of net required will vary a little as experimentation is needed in this area. The front section of the banner is attached to a sheer fabric to hold it in shape, but it is necessary to choose the finest fabric you can find. Fine nylon curtain material is strong and effective.

Required Materials

- ✓ 1 $^1/_2$ yards each of black, gold, nylon, muslin, black net and white net, 45 inches wide
- ✓ 1 $^3/_4$ yards deep blue ($^1/_4$ yard for trim in step 9), 45 inches wide
- ✓ 2 $^1/_2$ yards iron-on interfacing
- ✓ 6 yards silver cord
- ✓ 2 $^1/_2$ yards curtain tape
- ✓ Black wool or cord
- ✓ 1 dowel 44 inches long
- ✓ Glitter and sequins
- ✓ Glue gun, fabric glue and the usual sewing aids

Instructions

1. Enlarge design.
2. Trace onto iron-on interfacing, shiny side up, and cut out center of design.
3. Iron interfacing onto blue fabric and cut out center "light" portion.
4. Trace figures onto second piece of interfacing, iron onto wrong side of black fabric and cut out.
5. Using layers of black and white net, grade color of figures from dark to light.
6. Attach layers of net to each figure by stitching close to the edge. Trim net to figure size.
7. Glue or stitch figures onto blue fabric.
8. Outline figures with black wool.
9. Place this front section on the sheer nylon fabric. Cut nylon to exact size and pin together. Stitch around center outline and trim with silver cord. Bind both sides and lower edge with blue fabric.
10. Sew curtain tape along top edge.
11. Make back section of banner by joining gold fabric and muslin together.
12. Make a casing at the bottom that is large enough to hold a small dowel to weigh down the section.
13. Attach curtain tape to top edge.
14. Decorate gold fabric with glitter and sequins.
15. Hang completed banner where the lighting will emphasize the gold and glitter.

14

"The virgin will be with child and will give birth to a son, and they will call him Immanuel" — which means, "God with us."
— Matthew 1:23

Christmas and Epiphany

This set of banners fulfilled a vision to cover nearly the entire sanctuary wall of our small church, as a colorful contribution to the celebration and worship at Christmastide and into the season of Epiphany.

The banners are constructed by machine, but the fabric designs and trimmings are all glued. The red borders give a sense of uniformity, while parts of the design break out of the banner to emphasize the excitement and joy with which we celebrate Christmas.

The color choice is personal, relying on availability. However, it is necessary to keep in mind the wealth and riches of the wise men (kings), the earthiness of the shepherds, the fact that the angel is the heavenly messenger, and although the stable was definitely a very basic accommodation, Jesus is God's own son. Hence the use of gold.

The size of the banners can be adjusted to make the most of the available space. The photographed set measurements are:

Mary, Joseph and Jesus	48 inches by 48 inches
Angel	18 inches by 54 inches
Shepherds	27 inches by 39 inches
Star	24 inches by 18 inches
Wise Man	18 inches by 54 inches
Wise Men	27 inches by 60 inches

Required Materials

To make all banners in the specified sizes, you will need the following:

- ✓ Background fabric: 4 ½ yards
- ✓ Backing fabric: 4 ½ yards
- ✓ Border fabric: 1 ¾ yards
- ✓ Large selection of fabric for design
- ✓ Buckram or *very* stiff compressed batting
- ✓ Heavyweight iron-on interfacing
- ✓ Metallic trim, braid and wool for outlining
- ✓ Fabric or wood glue
- ✓ Clear adhesive (tube) or glue gun
- ✓ Dowels
- ✓ Brass eyes (small and medium-sized)
- ✓ Nylon fishing line

Instructions

Central Banner (Mary, Joseph and Jesus)

1. Enlarge design as explained on page 5.
2. Trace full-sized pattern onto iron-on interfacing, shiny side up, and also onto background fabric.
3. Select fabrics for the design, considering the overall effect and not just the individual banner. Spend time experimenting with colors and textures.
4. a. Iron selected fabric onto appropriate pieces of interfacing.
   b. When cutting pieces of pattern that go right to the edge of the banner, allow an extra $1/2$ inch to include in seam when constructing banner. (This applies only to the central banner.)
5. Cut background and backing fabrics to size, allowing a border of $1/2$ inch of extra material all around.
6. Cut border fabric into strips 4 inches wide. Sew this in place on background.
7. Glue into position the pieces of pattern that overlap the border and extend right to the edge of banner.
8. Attach hanging sleeves to the back of the banner.
9. Construct banner by placing background and backing right sides together. Sew around edge allowing $1/2$-inch seam, leaving just enough open to turn banner right side out. Trim seam allowance, turn, iron and topstitch $1/4$ inch from edge.
10. Now glue the remaining pattern pieces onto the background, fitting the pieces together like a jigsaw puzzle.
11. With a tube of clear adhesive or a glue gun, glue wool, braid or suitable trimming over outlines and places where fabrics meet.

Remaining Banners

Follow directions for central banner, omitting steps 4b and 7. Where design extends over the edge of the banner, sew buckram or compressed batting along the topstitch line. Glue pattern pieces onto the buckram. After gluing down suitable trimming, cut away surplus buckram or batting.

Hanging Banners

Cut dowels slightly narrower than completed banners and screw small brass eyes into the ends. Thread into hanging sleeves. Hang with nylon fishing line from brass eyes screwed into the ceiling or a suitable ledge. Adjust height and spacing to give the most pleasing effect in the space you have available. Admire and enjoy your completed project.

"While they were there, the time came for the baby to be born,
and she gave birth to her firstborn, a son." Luke 2:6-7a

"But the angel said to them, 'Do not be afraid. I bring you good news of great joy that will be for all the people.'"
— Luke 2:10

"We saw his star in the east and have come to worship him."
— Matthew 2:2b

"The shepherds said to one another, 'Let's go to Bethlehem and see this thing that has happened, which the Lord has told us about.'"
— Luke 2:15b

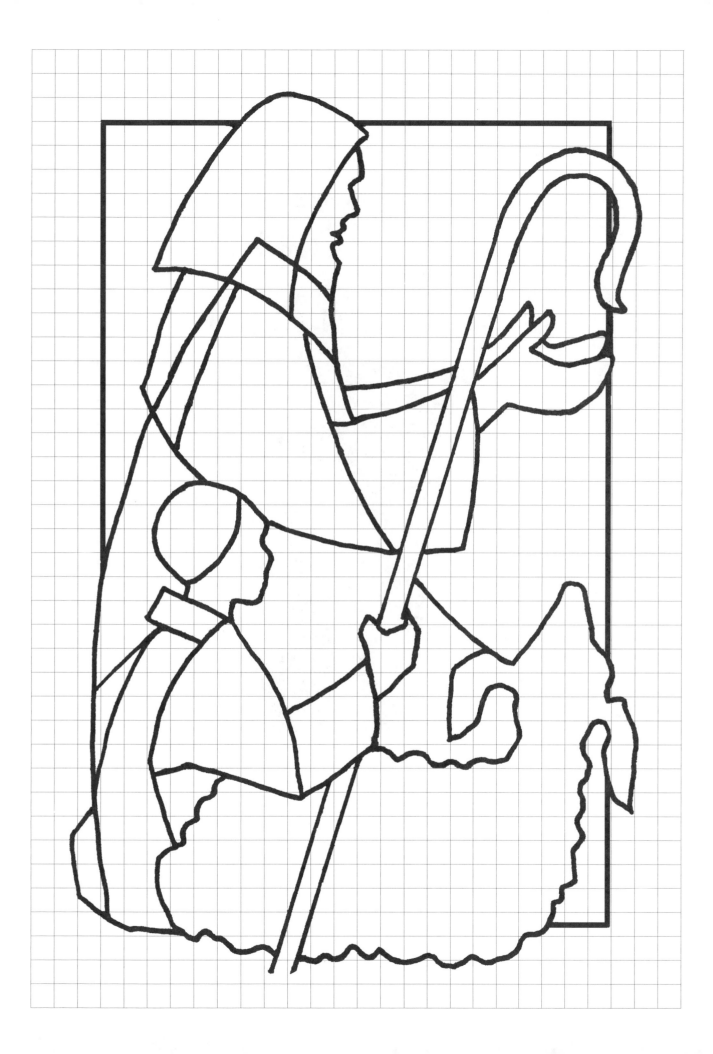

"On coming to the house, they saw the child
with his mother Mary, and they bowed down
and worshipped him. Then they presented him
with gifts of gold and of incense and of myrrh."
— Matthew 2:10 & 11

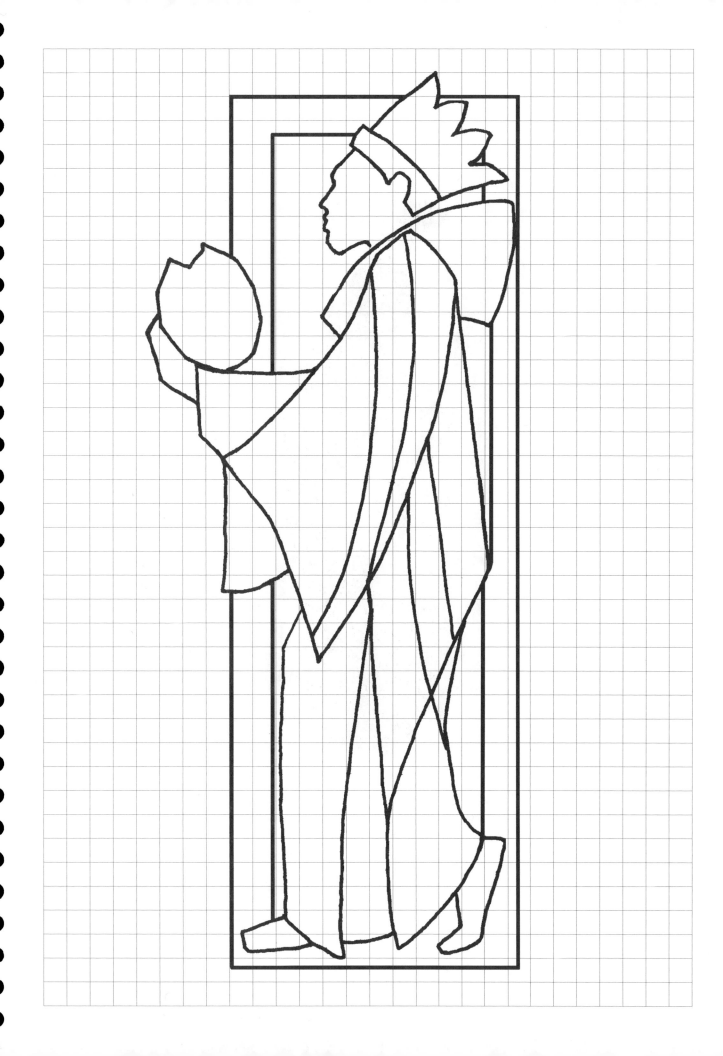

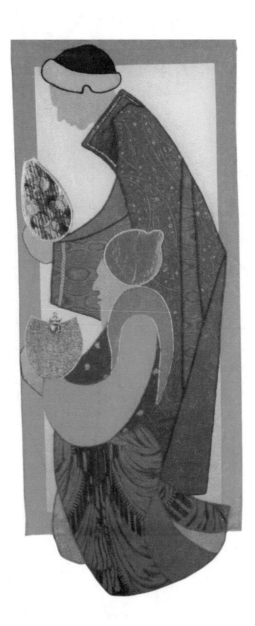

"On coming to the house, they saw the child with
his mother Mary, and they bowed down and
worshipped him. Then they presented him with gifts
of gold and of incense and of myrrh."
— Matthew 2:10 & 11

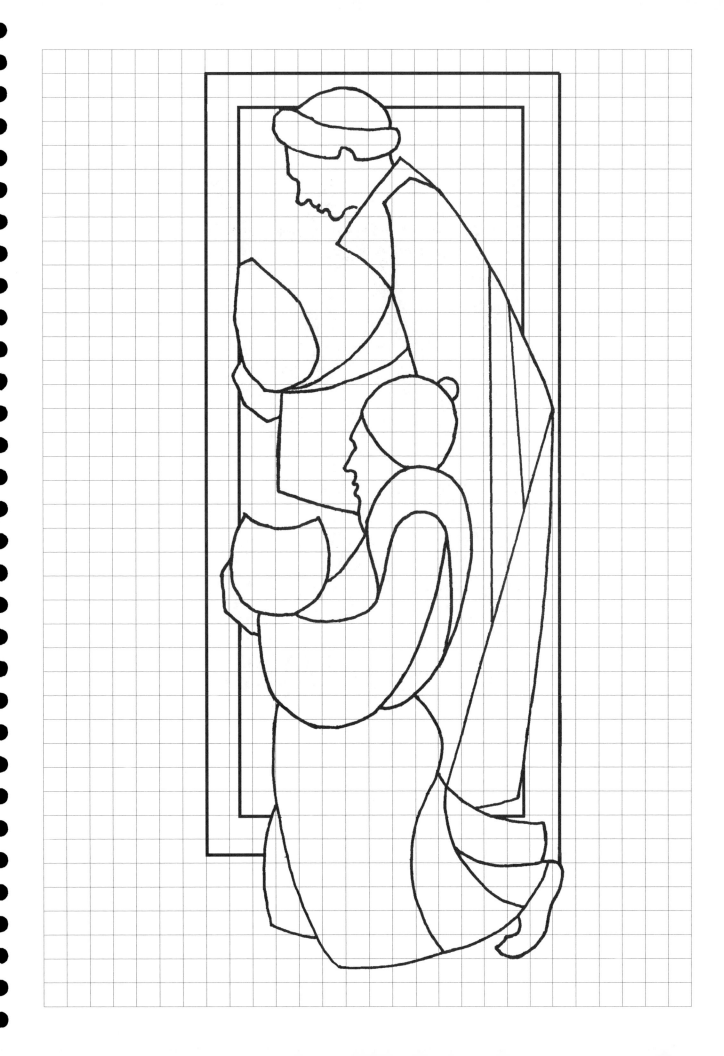

"Then a cloud appeared and enveloped them, and a voice came from the cloud: 'This is my Son, whom I love. Listen to him!'"
— Mark 9:7

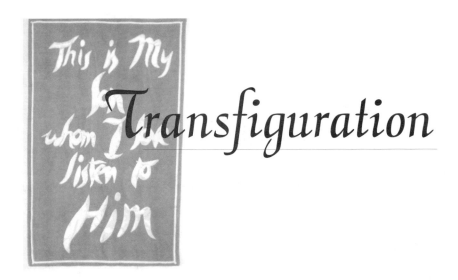

Transfiguration

This banner was designed to celebrate the Transfiguration and could also be used for the baptism of Jesus, as God used the same words on both occasions. The photographed banner was made using a velvet finish upholstery fabric for the background, which gives a very rich appearance, emphasizing the richness in the meaning of the text. The silver lettering, trim and hanging rod add to this theme. The finished size of the banner is 33 inches by 56 inches.

Required Materials

- ✓ 1 yard background fabric (velvet finish upholstery fabric)
- ✓ 1 yard backing fabric
- ✓ 1 yard lettering fabric
- ✓ 1 yard iron-on interfacing
- ✓ Cord or wool to outline lettering
- ✓ Braid
- ✓ Glue gun, fabric glue and the usual sewing aids
- ✓ Hanging rod and dowel for bottom of banner

Instructions

1. Enlarge lettering to fit the size of your banner.
2. Trace letters onto iron-on interfacing, shiny side up.
3. Cut out lettering and iron onto selected fabric.
4. Cut out and, using the graph as a guide, place letters on the background fabric. Be sure to hang your banner up at this point to check your lettering placement.
5. When you are happy with the lettering arrangement, glue or machine-appliqué in place.
6. Glue the cord around the outside of the letters, checking the graph carefully where letters overlap.
7. Construct the banner by sewing background and backing fabrics right sides together, leaving one end open to turn. Finish off by hand or machine. Add a sleeve at the lower edge so a rod can be concealed to add weight.
8. Make hanging loops and attach.
9. Glue or sew braid in place to frame the lettering.
10. Hang your banner on a suitably colored rod. Wooden rods can easily be spray painted to complement your banner.

"At that time Jesus came from Nazareth in Galilee and was
baptized by John in the Jordan. As Jesus was coming up out of
the water, he saw heaven being torn open and the Spirit
descending on him like a dove."
— Mark 1:9-10

Baptism

The design for this banner is self-explanatory, having used the Mark Scripture as a departure point. Our finished banner measured 36 inches by 40 inches.

The color moves from blue, symbolic of heaven and the Holy Spirit, into green/blue (symbolic of life, growth and purity). The movement of the dove descending also divides and tears (verse 10) the design in two. Yet the divisions of color do not disturb the composition. The effect of running water is continued by the use of large tassels attached to the bottom of the design.

Different textured material and overlays of net are used to create the color change from blue to green. Both sides of the same materials are also used. Silver ribbon, braid and sequins add flashes of light as sunlight would reflect on running water.

The colors were chosen from my scrap box, so each banner would vary according to the odds and ends you have collected. Adjust colors of sequins to materials chosen. Glitter glue in various colors was used to add glitz and excitement, and to increase the suggestion of movement. Tassels add length and the feeling of flowing water. Each is made from a ball of wool and some silver crochet cotton (two balls of silver were sufficient).

We trust that you will enjoy assembling the different colored materials and adding the bits and pieces of braid and sequins as much as we have.

Required Materials

- ✓ 1 ¼ yard muslin or white strong cotton material (just larger than template)
- ✓ 1 ¼ yard quilt batting (the size of your template)
- ✓ 1 ¼ yard iron-on interfacing
- ✓ Various materials from scrap box
- ✓ Two balls silver crochet cotton
- ✓ Five balls of wool to match your design colors
- ✓ Approximately 20 yards silver and gold braid
- ✓ Sequins in various colors
- ✓ Glue gun, fabric glue and the usual sewing aids
- ✓ Suitable dowel and paint

Instructions

1. The construction is outlined in the Basic Technique section on pages 5 and 6.
2. Trace shapes onto iron-on interfacing (shiny side up) and cut out.
3. Iron onto selected fabric and cut out.
4. Cut batting into the banner shape using your full-sized template. This facilitates assembly.
5. Attach the batting to the muslin backing material with glue.
6. Assemble shapes onto the quilt batting and pin into place.
7. Hold up and check to see if there is a good gradation of color. Once satisfied, glue to batting/backing.
8. Make five 16-inch tassels with silver crochet cotton and balls of wool.
9. Use glue gun to attach braids.
10. Glue or sew sequins, using various colors.
11. Make hanging loops from ³/₄-inch-wide silver braid.
12. The dowel used in the original banner pictured here is a discarded broom stick found in my kitchen cupboard. It is painted blue with a water-based paint.
13. Certain areas of the banner were painted with Dazzle appliqué glue to add sparkle. Appliqué glue also changes the face of the fabric and adds interest.

Details of baptism banner.

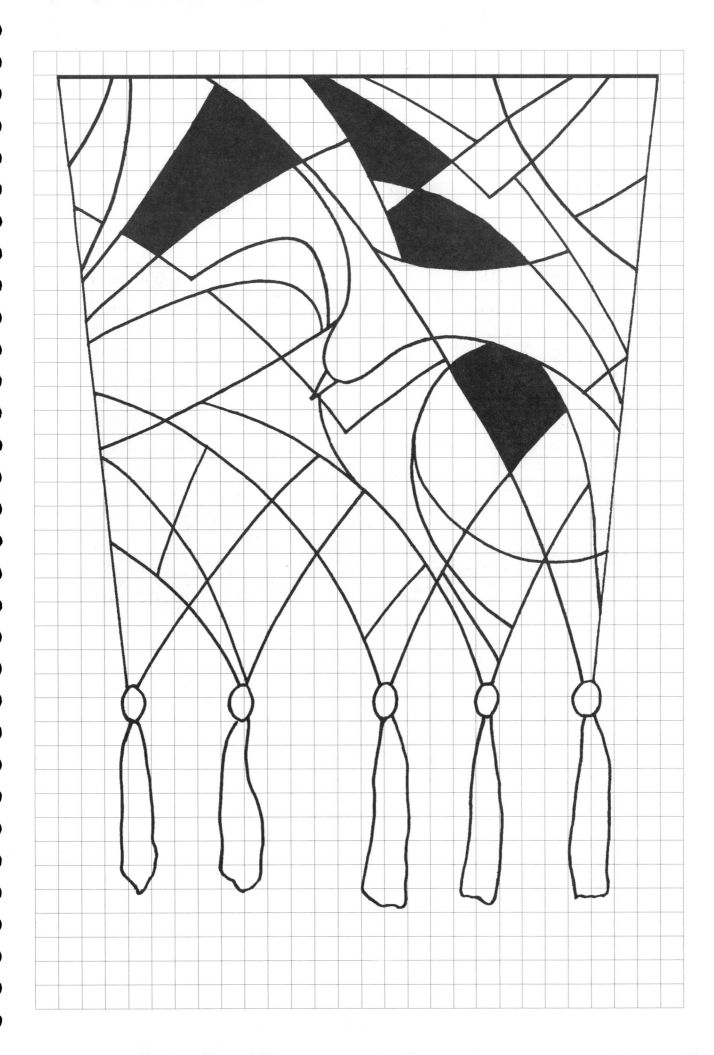

"One of the soldiers pierced Jesus' side with a spear,
bringing a sudden flow of blood and water."
— John 19:34

The Lenten season is a time when Christians are challenged to self-examination corporately and individually. This should culminate in the seeking of restitution and forgiveness. The symbolism of the altar frontal is taken from the John 19 scripture. It represents one of the final acts of Jesus in washing away our sins by his blood and living water while yet in this world. Our finished banner measured 120 inches by 34 inches.

The silver and white Canterbury cross is representative of Christ surrounded by a silver and blue circular background symbolizing the world. The sweeping movement in the design is indicative of flowing water. The red represents the blood, and blue represents the water that flowed from Christ's side. These cut through the rest of the design, dividing the darkness represented by the traditional colors of the remainder of the frontal.

When choosing the colors for this frontal, be conscious of the spot where it is to hang. It was designed for a church with fairly dark brick walls. This meant that the purple and blue fabrics could be chosen in light shades as there was very little reflected light. If your church has better lighting, retain the emotive quality of the frontal by selecting darker shades of purple and blue.

The frontal could easily be altered to a banner format. Hanging loops could be attached to the top. It could also be made in sections. Lettering in silver and gold would also be appropriate. Follow the flow of the design when using lettering. The scripture used at the beginning of the chapter would be suitable.

A variety of fabrics such as velvet, cotton, satin and lamé were color-coordinated to enhance the deep significance of the Lenten season. There is a fair amount of wastage as none of the fabrics were joined. This was purposely done to retain the fluidity of the design. Keep all scraps for future works. To measure the lengths of materials to be used for the frontal, use the full-scale template. When we were purchasing the fabrics for our frontal, we were bold enough to take the template shopping with us. Most shop personnel were amused but very helpful in assisting with selections.

Use the template to establish how much braid is needed. Use different thicknesses and textured braid to add interest to your design. Glitter glue and sequins are used in strategic areas to catch and reflect light. The decorative aids help to focus and retain your attention when working with larger areas.

When tackling a banner or frontal of this size, make sure you have a conducive working area. Cramped space and an inadequate working surface will only cause frustration. A corner of our church hall was made available to us and proved to be a great blessing as the studio was too small to accommodate this work.

Required Materials

✓ Backing material (muslin or white cotton) just larger than template

✓ Quilt batting (the size of your template)

✓ A variety of color-coordinated fabrics (such as velvet, cotton, satin and lamé)

✓ Sequins, glitter glue, pearl beads

✓ Black braid in different textures and thicknesses

✓ Muslin or white cotton to cover the top surface of the altar, plus 10 inches for overhang

✓ A heavy dowel the length of the altar

✓ Glue gun, fabric glue and the usual sewing aids

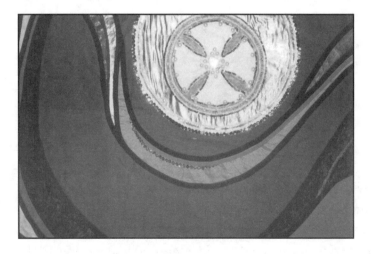

Detail of Lenten altar frontal

Instructions

1. This altar frontal is constructed in the manner described on pages 5 and 6.

2. Certain areas are slightly padded using quilt batting. This was incorporated to add interest to the face of the frontal, as it covers a large area. Cut and glue down the batting onto the backing cloth. As it is lightweight, you could pad the entire area of the frontal if you wish.

3. Assemble shapes onto the quilt batting and pin into place.

4. Glue or sew on black braid to separate each color. This adds visual impact and enhances the emotive quality of the work.

5. Construct the cross using heavy pearl beads. We sewed the beads on by hand as our frontal is moved and stored away several times a year. Use double thread for the beads, as well as the sequins and the braid surrounding the cross. (A glue gun was used to attach the black braid.)

6. Glue or sew on black braid along the edge of the banner, which confines the design and prevents the imagery from "floating."

7. Once the frontal is complete, stitch a length of white cloth to the top edge. It should be wide enough to cover the top of the altar plus 10 inches for an overhang. Sew a casing along the edge of the overhang into which a dowel is inserted. This added weight keeps the frontal in place. (In our church, we have metal rods for this purpose.)

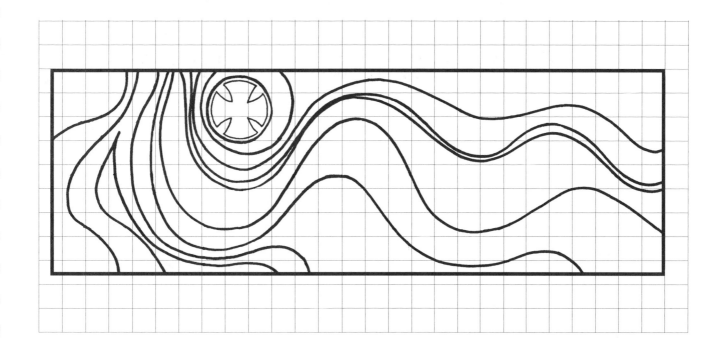

"A very large crowd spread their cloaks on the road, while others cut branches from trees and spread them on the road. The crowds that went ahead of him and those that followed shouted, 'Hosanna to the son of David. Blessed is he who comes in the name of the Lord. Hosanna in the highest!'"
— Matthew 21:8-9

Palm Sunday

This banner to celebrate the Triumphal Entry of Jesus into Jerusalem gives opportunity for each banner maker or banner-making group to make their own interpretation. Our finished banner measured 80 inches by 54 inches.

You will need a suitable heavy cotton fabric for the background which will be colored with a sun (heliographic) paint technique. I used cream fabric for the figures, outlining with different colored wools, but there is no reason why the crowd could not be multicolored. A little gray and white fabric will be required for Jesus and the donkey, and you will also need strong fabric for the "prairie point" border. A small amount of fabric for lettering and a backing fabric are also required.

Although this banner is designed with Palm Sunday in mind, it is a happy banner that will give pleasure and could be used for other celebrations.

Required Materials

✓ 2 ¼ yards backing fabric (muslin)

✓ 2 ¼ yards background fabric (preferably white)

✓ Heavy iron-on interfacing

✓ Fabrics for all figures, letters, border and hanging tabs

✓ Sun paints (Setacolor fabric paint by Pebeo is available from Dharma Trading Company, 1-800-542-5227, dharmatrading.com/setacolor.html)

✓ Wool or braid for outlining

✓ Suitable dowel

✓ Glue gun, fabric glue and the usual sewing aids

Instructions

1. Decide on the completed size of your banner and cut background and backing fabrics slightly larger.
2. Sun paint background fabric
   a. Select sun paint colors in various shades of green and blue.
   b. From magazine paper, cut enough leaf and jacket templates in several different shapes to cover fabric.
   c. Wet fabric, dip into sun paint and spread on the lawn in full sunlight. Splash different colored sun paints in different areas to add interest.
   d. Lay paper templates on wet fabric and leave to dry in the sun. The dyeing process takes place as the fabric dries. Once dry, remove paper templates. Your material is now ready to begin your banner.
3. Enlarge the design of Jesus and the donkey. Trace onto iron-on interfacing, cut out and iron onto fabric.
4. Cut patterns of simple people in several different sizes and trace onto iron-on interfacing. Cut out and iron onto selected fabrics. Arrange to form a crowd around Jesus and the donkey as pleases your eye.
5. Glue figures in place and outline with wool or braid.
6. Cut lettering for acclamations from fabrics that complement your particular sun paints. Arrange around the palm and jacket design in the background and glue in place.
7. With a black felt tip marker, draw in a few extra figures and add feet to some of the fabric figures, to add to the "crowd" effect.
8. Make "prairie points" for the border by cutting long strips of fabric 6 inches wide. Fold in half lengthwise and iron flat. Cut into 6-inch pieces and fold into triangles. Secure these around the outside edge and back your banner.
9. Cut hanging loops of the same fabric as the "prairie points" and attach to upper edge of banner.

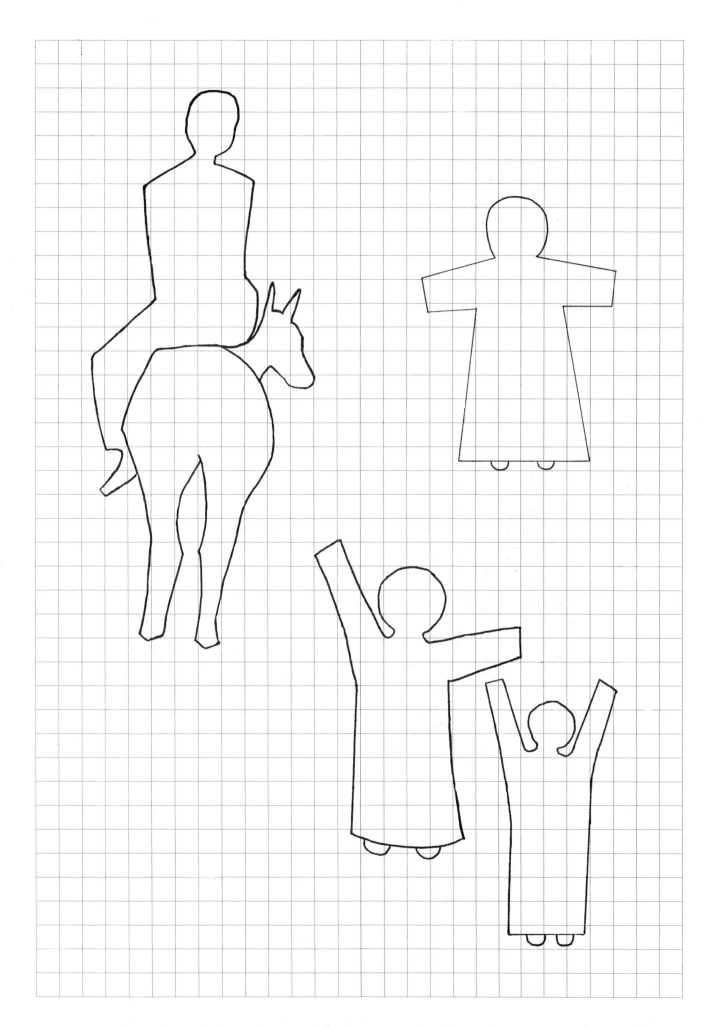

"At that moment the curtain of the temple
was torn in two from top to bottom."
— Matthew 27:51

Good Friday

This banner has been designed using the technique of "colorwash quilts," but with a greater freedom than normally governs this style of patchwork. Fabrics have been repeated with far more regularity, and plain fabrics have been used in and around the cross to produce a greater impact. The banner is made up of a series of little squares, sewn together to create an illusion of the Matthew Scripture. Our banner measured 21 inches by 25 ½ inches.

Depicted is the cross of Jesus breaking through the veil into the Holy of Holies. To the people of Israel, the Holy of Holies was the dwelling place or throne of God on earth. Gold covered the Ark of the Covenant with the cherubim watching over it, and this sacred place was resplendent with the glory of God. The high priest only entered the Holy of Holies once a year, wearing fine linen garments of purple, blue and red. The curtain, which was made of the same fabric as the priest's garments (Exodus 26:31 and 28:5), was rent from top to bottom on that first Good Friday, so the Holy of Holies was opened for all to enter. It is into this place the banner is inviting you.

Required Materials

✓ Large piece of polystyrene covered with a soft fabric to which other fabrics will cling

✓ Small pieces of a large selection of fabrics

✓ Velvet or satin ribbon

✓ 1 yard lightweight quilt batting

✓ 1 yard backing fabric (muslin)

✓ Metallic thread for quilting

✓ 2 brass rods

✓ 8 brass curtain rings

✓ 16 gold/brass buttons

Instructions

1. Cut fabric into 2-inch squares for the main part of the banner. The fabric squares to be used in the cross are smaller (1-inch square) with four small squares forming one 2-inch square.

2. Begin by arranging fabric squares on the board, relying on your eye to guide you to the most pleasing placing. The squares are placed "on point" and are ultimately sewn together in diagonal rows. When satisfied with any particular section, pin those squares to the board to secure. Continue section by section until you have completed the entire banner area. Remember that the completed banner will be much smaller when all the seams have been sewn.

3. Now position your board where you can glance at it frequently — especially as you walk into a room, where it can "surprise" you. Reshuffle, twist and turn squares until you feel satisfied with your design. This process could go on forever, so it is essential to set yourself a deadline and begin sewing at 9 a.m. on Tuesday!

4. Sew pieces in diagonal rows, using $^1/_4$-inch seam allowance.

5. When sewing is completed, mark radiating quilting lines.

6. Tack together backing, batting and banner design.

7. Machine quilt, preferably with metallic thread.

8. Bind banner, using a light color at the top and a toning, darker one around the lower section.

9. Attach hanging loops at top and bottom.

10. Placing two different color ribbons together, attach to curtain rings with buttons. Thread banner loops and curtain rings onto top brass rod. Twist ribbons and secure to bottom of banner with buttons, placing in such a way as to emphasize the tearing of the temple curtain from top to bottom. Thread bottom loops onto the brass rod and hang your completed banner.

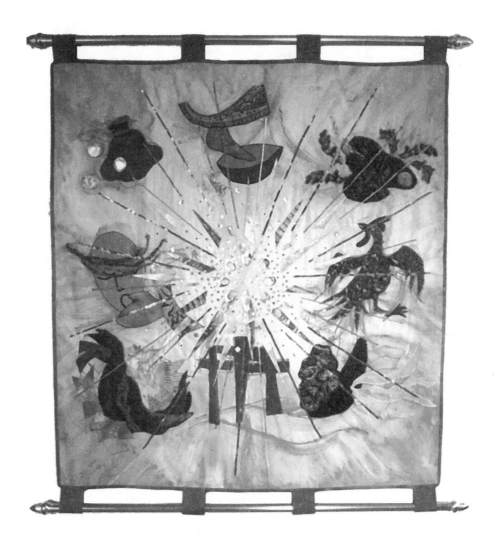

"He has risen from the dead"
— Matthew 28:7

Easter

In this banner we have tried to depict the resurrection of Jesus as an explosion of life that overcame all that had preceded the Crucifixion. The background fabric has been dyed to accentuate the central explosion, with some of the events leading up to the Resurrection appliquéd onto it. The radiating central design needs to express the victory of Jesus overcoming death, the light overcoming the darkness. To emphasize this, upper and lower hanging rods are used.

The size of this banner can be determined by the amount of space you have available, and fabric quantities may be worked out accordingly. Our finished banner measured 41 inches by 44 inches.

The following Scriptures were the inspiration for the pre-Resurrection motifs.

1. "Then one of the twelve — the one called Judas Iscariot — went to the chief priests and asked, 'What are you willing to give me if I hand him over to you?' So they counted out for him thirty pieces of silver." Matthew 26:14 and 15

2. "After that, he poured water into a basin and began to wash his disciples' feet." John 13:5

3. "'Could you not keep watch with me for one hour?' he asked Peter." Matthew 26:40

4. "Then they spat in his face and struck him with their fists." Matthew 26:67

5. "'I tell you the truth, before the cock crows, you will disown me three times!'" John 13:38

6. "The soldiers twisted together a crown of thorns and put it on his head. They clothed him in a purple robe." John 19:2

7. "Here they crucified him, and with him two others." John 19:18

8. "Mary Magdalene went to the tomb and saw that the stone had been removed from the entrance ... He bent over and looked in at the strips of linen lying there." John 20:1 and 5

Required Materials

✓   1 ¹/₂ yards background fabric (white), 45 inches wide

✓   Fabric dyes

✓   1 ¹/₂ yards muslin or other suitable backing fabric

✓   Red fabric for binding and hanging loops

✓   Iron-on interfacing

✓   Selection of small pieces of fabric

✓   Wool cord for outlining

✓   Selection of gold fabric, cords and braids

✓   Sequins

✓   Glue gun, fabric glue and the usual sewing aids

✓   2 brass rods for hanging

Detail of rooster crowing.

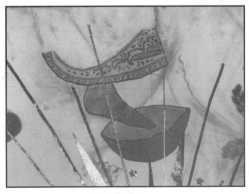

Detail of foot washing.

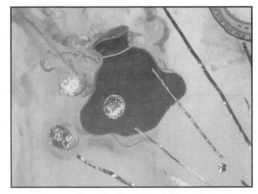

Detail of money bag.

Instructions

1. Having decided on the size of your banner, tie-dye a square of background fabric in orange and yellow dyes.

2. Select the fabric for the eight motifs and place the motifs on the background. Some of the fabric will require interfacing, while in other places a better effect will be achieved by placing and draping suitable pieces of fabric. These motifs can be glued or hand- or machine-appliquéd in place. Outline with wool or cord where necessary.

3. When you are satisfied with your motifs, construct your banner by binding the background and backing fabric together with the red fabric. Attach hanging loops at the top and bottom.

4. Now arrange pieces of fabric, cord, braid and sequins until you have the desired explosive effect. Keep hanging your banner to check as you go along. You may find yourself adding to this long after you have considered your banner complete.

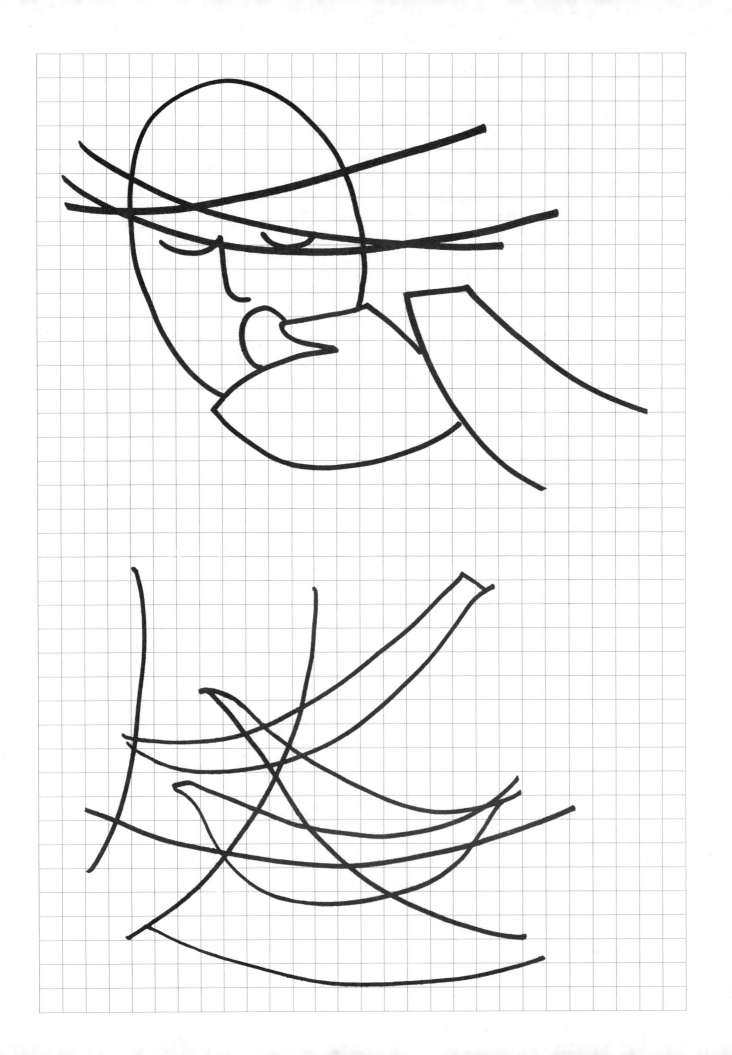

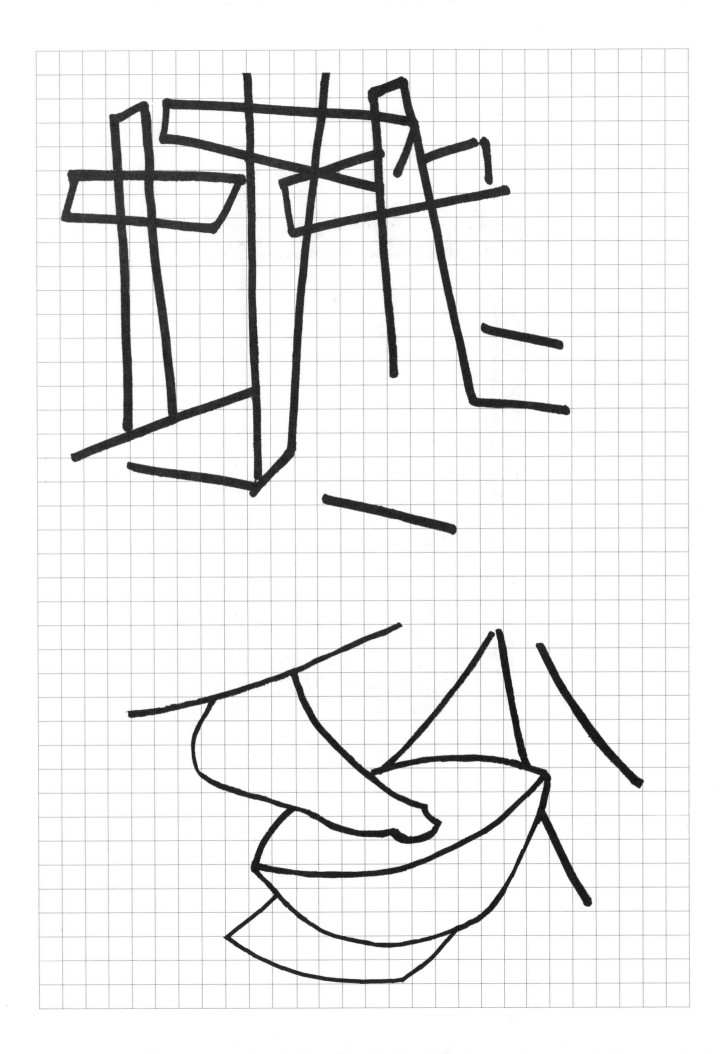

"While he was blessing them, he left them
and was taken up into heaven."
—Luke 24:51

Ascension

This banner design is a figurative interpretation of the Luke Scripture. Christ is seen as a free-floating figure with people below. Their arms are outstretched in an attitude of worship.

I deliberately chose to give the design a pseudo-African character. A loosely woven cotton was used throughout the banner. This material is used for traditional costuming by the local Xhosa people. Much of their clothing is also decorated with black braid. The decorative border was loosely based on local beadwork designs of South Africa. Color was added by applying ordinary wax crayons. Once an area was colored in, it was ironed to prevent the colors from spreading. Before ironing, those areas were covered by unprinted newsprint. The worshipping figures were painted in using black fabric paint. Thick black wool in a single strand was used to outline the figure of Christ and the vegetation. This was glued on using a glue gun. Large wooden beads are added to the bottom of the banner as a finishing touch.

The size of this banner will be determined by the area where it will hang. Increase or decrease the grid size when drawing out the template to suit your needs. Our banner measured 32 inches by 60 inches.

This design can easily be adapted and adjusted to be given a local or traditional ethos. Peruvian braid designs or Mexican embroidery patterns could look really stunning as a border design. Adjustments to the color could also be made.

Required Materials

- ✓ Cream-colored cotton of a loose weave (just larger than your template size)
- ✓ Backing cloth to match the above, i.e., denim
- ✓ Black braid
- ✓ Black wool
- ✓ Wax crayons
- ✓ Fabric paint
- ✓ Large wood beads
- ✓ Wooden rod for hanging
- ✓ Glue gun, fabric glue and the usual sewing aids

Instructions

1. Once you have completed your template, trace your design onto the cream-colored cotton.

2. Using fabric paint, paint in the worshipping figures and border design. Make sure the paint is completely dry before moving onto the next step.

3. Now proceed with the coloring-in with wax crayons. Do not forget to iron after each color has been completed, as the colors can easily smudge. Children may be recruited to help at this stage.

4. Once the coloring-in of the design has been completed, proceed by outlining the figure of Christ, the lettering and the vegetation using black wool. Use your glue gun for this task.

5. Glue down black braid to frame the border pattern.

6. Either slip-stitch the backing cloth onto the banner, turning the edges in, or use your sewing machine.

7. Hand stitch wooden beads to the bottom and braid loops to the top of banner.

8. A plain wooden dowel may be used to hang the banner. Give it a coat of paint or decorate it in some way if desired.

Detail of Ascension banner.

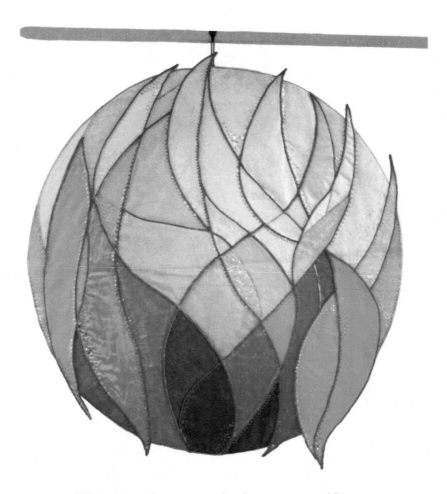

"They saw what seemed to be tongues of fire
that separated and came to rest on each of them."
— Acts 2:3

Pentecost

The Pentecost design is an interpretation of a dream Joyce had — the desire of God's heart for the Holy Spirit to enfold the whole earth. As she talked, Anne sketched, and the imagery and shapes grew simultaneously. We had a wonderful time brainstorming and interpreting the design. A huge three-dimensional ball of large proportions hanging from a church ceiling was considered. Another idea was for the banner to be carried into church on a sturdy pole with ribbons attached to the back. Dancers would hold the ends and dance behind the banner as it processed up the aisle.

The materials used were mostly pieces found in our scrap box. If a color needed adjustment, it was dyed darker. Overlaying with nets and transparent nylons created texture and color.

We created our own braid by crocheting together (using a continuous daisy-chain stitch) two gold crochet cotton threads with red wool yarn. One standard-sized ball of wool was adequate to complete the banner. Gold ribbon of various lengths and braid was also used.

For the banner to keep its shape, a semi-circle was cut from plywood to fit in the upper half of the material circle.

We enjoyed the reaction of various friends and congregation members to this banner. The shape has also inspired members to a new insight into the work of the Holy Spirit.

The finished banner is about $1\frac{1}{2}$ yards in diameter. A 6-inch grid size was used. When enlarging the design, the area in which you choose to display it will ultimately dictate the final size.

Required Materials

- ✓ 3 ¼ yards light-colored heavy-duty cotton or denim
- ✓ Plywood (for board shape)
- ✓ 1 ½ yards quilt batting
- ✓ Light-colored felt-tip pen
- ✓ Various material scraps
- ✓ Various scraps of net and transparent nylon
- ✓ 1 ball gold crochet cotton
- ✓ 1 ball 14-ply red wool yarn
- ✓ Gold ribbon
- ✓ Braid
- ✓ Sequins — transparent, pearly and opaque
- ✓ Hook for hanging banner
- ✓ Glue gun, fabric glue and the usual sewing aids

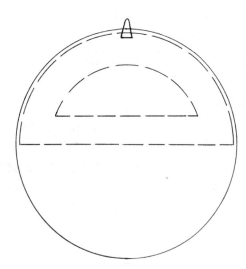

Plywood board shape

Detail of Pentecost banner

Instructions

1. Cut the heavy-duty cotton into circular shapes the size of your template. Machine stitch the two pieces together to half the diameter. Leave a small opening at the top end. Turn right side out.

2. Cut a semi-circle from the plywood to fit in the cotton circle. To lighten the weight, cut out the center of the plywood piece using a jigsaw. At the top-most point, attach a sturdy hook to facilitate the hanging of the finished work.

3. Slip the cotton circle over the half-moon plywood shape. The hook will protrude from the opening left at the top. Find an area of wall space to hang it.

4. Place the quilt batting on the full-scale template. Using a light-colored felt-tipped pen, trace the flame shapes onto the batting. Cut and reassemble the shapes and pin onto the circle of heavy-duty cotton.

5. Once the shapes have been arranged as per designs from the template, start adding color. Select suitable materials and colors, keeping in mind the texture and character of flames of fire. Each flame shape is individually covered and reassembled onto the circle of cotton. Use fabric glue to attach the materials to the batting.

6. Once you are satisfied that you have a good progression of color characteristic of rising flames, glue the shapes to the cotton. Use a glue gun for this purpose.

7. Trim flames with red and gold chord, braid and ribbon. Your glue gun can be used for this task. You can either stitch or glue on sequins. This final touch adds life to the flames. We chose to stitch the sequins, as the banner would be moved and stored several times during the calendar year.

8. Finally, turn in the seam of the lower half of the banner. Slip stitch the two halves together.

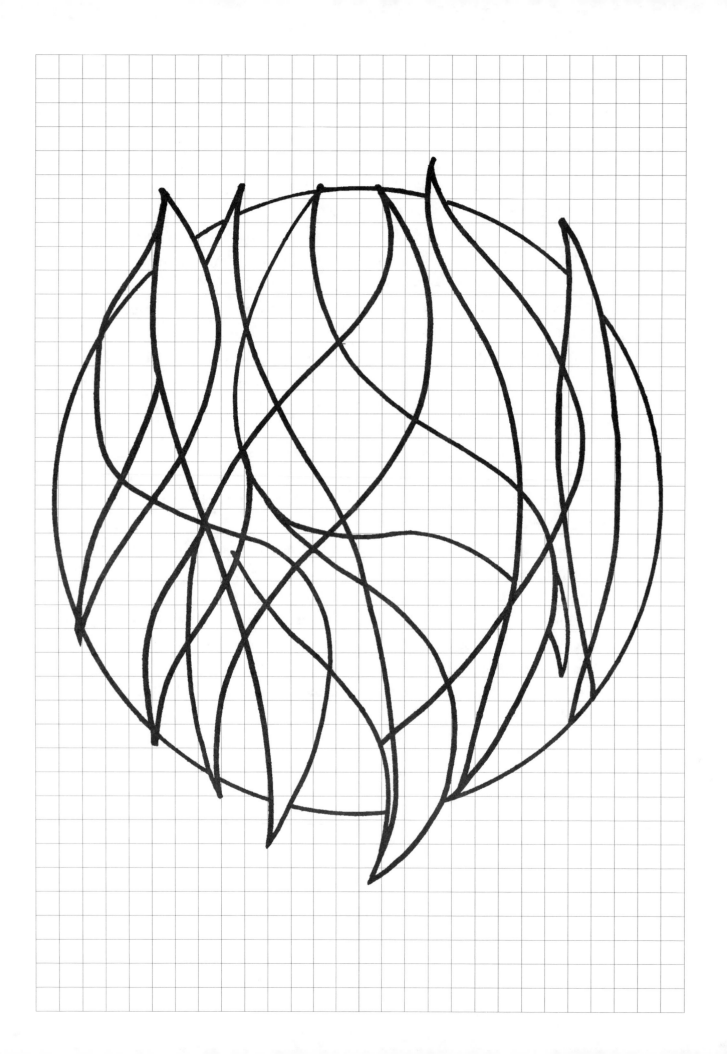

70

"Jesus said, 'But the counselor, the Holy Spirit, whom
the Father will send in my name, will teach you all things
and will remind you of everything I have said to you.'"
— John 14:26

Trinity Sunday

This "three-in-one" banner has been designed with the patchworker/quilter in mind, although these techniques may well be changed to suit your particular skills. The "flying geese" border could be replaced with a suitable braid, while the machine quilting used to accentuate the triangular lines could be omitted. Trinity Sunday would be a wonderful day to hang this banner, but it could have a more permanent position in a church, being the very basis of our Christian faith. The center panel on our finished banner measures 23 ½ inches by 70 inches. The side panels measure 20 inches by 64 inches.

This banner speaks through the symbols, relying very little on the words, and is therefore ideal for use in multi-language places of worship. In Africa or the East, where different-language congregations use the same building at different times, such a banner is ideal.

Symbols

THREE BANNERS to make up the whole depicts the three persons of the Godhead who make up the Trinity: Father, Son and Holy Spirit.

TRIANGLE: The three angles of the triangle combine to make one complete figure. It is commonly used as a symbol of the Trinity. This is endorsed in the triangular border.

CIRCLE: This represents eternity, having no beginning and no ending.

INTERTWINING CIRCLES: These circles depict the equality, unity and co-eternal nature of the Trinity.

TRUMPETS: Calling people to worship the Holy Trinity in the words of Isaiah 6:3, "Holy, holy, holy is the Lord Almighty; the whole earth is full of His glory."

HAND OF GOD: The hand of God pointing downward is a symbol of God the Father as the one who blesses his people. Three extended fingers suggest the Holy Trinity, while the two closed fingers show the two-fold nature of Jesus — fully human and fully God.

CROSS: This Greek cross has an X superimposed and represents God the son, Jesus. The X is the first letter of the Greek word for Christ.

DOVE: Represents God, the Holy Spirit.

The three symbols of the Godhead have been appliquéd onto the same background fabric and have been outlined with gold, emphasizing their importance. Blue, being the heavenly color, was chosen to dominate, as it speaks of divinity and grace.

Required Materials

✓ 4 yards background fabric, 45 inches wide

✓ A selection of cream fabrics for the hand, triangle, squares, circles and patchwork border

✓ Blue fabric

✓ 4 yards lightweight quilt batting

✓ 4 yards backing fabric

✓ Selection of wool, cord and braid

✓ Curtain rod and dowels for hanging

✓ Glue gun, fabric glue and the usual sewing aids

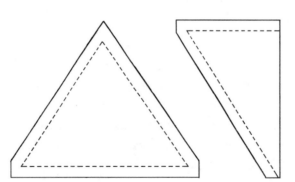

"Flying geese" border patterns

Detail of intertwining circles

Detail of cross

Instructions

1. Enlarge design as explained on page 5-7 of this book.
2. Trace symbols and words onto iron-on interfacing (shiny side up).
3. Select fabrics and iron interfacing designs onto fabric.
4. Cut out and place on background fabric.
5. Machine appliqué, being sure to work smaller pieces onto larger pieces, trimming and outlining as much as possible before attaching to the background. Outlining with wool, cord or braid gives a crisper finish, especially around the lettering.
6. Make the "flying geese" border, noting that the border within the main triangle is color-reversed.
7. Sew side borders in place first, followed by top and bottom strips, adjusting to fit with the plain fabric in the center.
8. If quilting, mark lines 2 inches apart on the background, following the triangular lines.
9. Cut batting and background fabric slightly larger than each banner. Sandwich the three layers together as for a quilt. Tack together and machine quilt with contrasting thread.
10. Stitch and trim banner edges.
11. Attach a sleeve for hanging at the top and another at the bottom of each banner before binding with $1\frac{1}{4}$-inch wide strips of fabric.
12. Hang banners on one long rod, being sure the distance between them gives accurate lines to the triangle. Put individual dowels through lower sleeves of each banner for weight.

"God, the blessed and only Ruler, the King of kings and Lord of lords,"
— 1 Timothy 6:15

Christ the King

This processional banner is designed to be carried by one banner bearer following the other into church or wherever your particular celebration is taking place. The design is identical on both sides, with the crown of thorns going ahead of the crown of glory.

It is a simple banner to make, but it can be time-consuming because of its size. The photographed example measures 3 ¼ yards long by 34 inches deep, and the fabric requirements listed are for that size. It will be necessary to choose a heavy fabric for the background to avoid the lettering showing through from one side to the other. Or, you can line the banner with muslin. This will also give the necessary weight for the banner to hang well. A processional banner needs to be sturdy to cope with the extra handling it endures. For this reason, it is wise to stitch the lettering in place. A strong, rich color for the lettering will have a greater impact, along with the matching fringe. The trimming to outline the lettering needs to be inexpensive, as many yards are required. Thick gold knitting yarn works well and is cost-effective.

Required Materials

✓ 6 ½ yards background fabric

✓ 6 ½ yards muslin (for optional lining)

✓ 2 ¼ yards lettering fabric

✓ 2 ¼ yards iron-on interfacing

✓ Lettering trim

✓ 13 yards fringe

✓ Brass rods approximately 60 inches long

✓ Glue gun, fabric glue and the usual sewing aids

Instructions

1. Enlarge lettering to required size.
2. Using stiff iron-on interfacing, trace letters, shiny side up, and cut out.
3. Iron onto the wrong side of chosen fabric. For a rich effect, velvet is wonderful, but special care must be taken when ironing on the interfacing.
4. Cut out letters and arrange on banner, being as accurate as possible with positioning and spacing.
5. Glue in place before sewing with a small zigzag stitch.
6. Glue trim, yarn or wool around letters.
7. If lining, pin muslin lining to backs of both banner sides.
8. With right sides together, stitch both ends and upper edge of banner together.
9. Turn, iron and top stitch.
10. Iron a ½-inch turn up along the lower edge to finish edge and top sew fringe to both sides of banner.
11. Make crowns using instructions on following page.
12. Position crowns on banner. Use Velcro to secure crowns to banner so they will be held firmly in place.
13. At both ends of the banner, do a row of stitching to form a tube for holding the rods.
14. Insert rods and position the crowns in readiness for two strong people to grandly lead the procession.

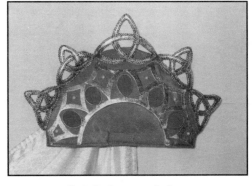

Detail of crown of glory

Detail of crown of thorns

Crowns

Most of the fabrics required for the crowns will be in your scrap drawer, as the colors used may be your own choice. We selected purple and gold because they are the royal colors; the red velvet depicts the blood that was shed for each one of us. Stiff iron-on interfacing will be required, plus a small amount of batting and several yards of gold trim to outline the Celtic design on the crown of glory. The crowns are made along the lines of a tea cozy, with the design on both sides.

Crown of Glory:
1. Enlarge design.
2. Trace the semicircle and the decorative design onto interfacing, shiny side up. Repeat this step for the second side of the crown.
3. Iron interfacing onto the selected fabrics and cut out, allowing for seams on the outer edges of the semicircle.
4. Glue or machine-appliqué lower design in place.
5. Cut batting and lining to fit semicircle and construct your crown, leaving three to four inches open on one side.
6. Hem lower edge and side opening.
7. Outline Celtic design with suitable braid, being careful to follow the under and over design.
8. Handstitch design in place on both sides of crown by catching at suitable places.
9. Glue upper parts of Celtic design together, carefully matching both sides.
10. Decorate lower design with pearls and glitzy trimmings as you desire.

Crown of Thorns:
The basic construction of this crown is the same as the Crown of Glory except for steps 2 and 7, and omitting step 10.

2. Trace the semicircle and the decorative design onto interfacing, shiny side up. Repeat this step for the second side of the crown, *being careful to reverse the thorn design for the second side.*
7. Embroider or outline thorns with wool or cord to give a sharp edge.

"I am the true vine and my Father is the gardener. He cuts off every
branch in me that bears no fruit, while every branch that does bear fruit
he prunes so that it will be even more fruitful. You are already clean
because of the word I have spoken to you. Remain in me, and I will
remain in you. No branch can bear fruit by itself; it must remain in the vine.
Neither can you bear fruit unless you remain in me.
I am the vine; you are the branches, if a man remains in me and I in him,
he will bear much fruit; apart from me you can do nothing."
— John 15 : 1-5

Green Season

The theme for this frontal is taken from the John Scripture. A loose design of vine leaves was sponged onto a cotton fabric, and three layers of transparent green cloth was draped and stitched across the face of the frontal.

When one approaches the frontal, the layers of green cloth flutter as the air stirs. This gives a vibrant sensation of being part of the vine and recalls the promise of our heavenly Father.

The colors you select to paint the frontal and overlays depend on personal interpretation. We chose to introduce warmer tones, as the altar stands on a green and blue carpet. Our finished frontal measured 120 inches by 34 inches, which is rather big. Don't let the size deter you from adapting it to one suitable for your own needs.

Required Materials

- ✓ 3 yards of thick, good-quality white cotton to paint on
- ✓ An extra length of cotton to cover the top surface of the altar, plus 10 inches to hang your frontal
- ✓ A heavy dowel the length of the altar
- ✓ A selection of fabric paints and sponges
- ✓ Sheets of medium weight card stock to make leaf stencils
- ✓ A hobby knife and scissors to cut card stock
- ✓ Three varying lengths of green material (Use a progression of shades graded from dark to light. The more transparent this cloth is, the more visible the leaf design behind it will become. This will enhance the idea of the vine being a living, growing organism.)
- ✓ Glue gun, fabric glue and the usual sewing aids

Instructions

1. Create your background by sponging paint around the edges of your leaf stencils. Use your paints according to their instructions. Transparent, water-based paint was used for our frontal. Enlarge the leaf template to various sizes and make stencils with card stock. (We used sizes from 20 inches to 8 inches.) Stenciling onto a wet background in areas prevents the design from becoming too rigid.

2. When you are satisfied with the painting, fix the material according to the instructions given with the paint.

3. Now cut your material to size, leaving an allowance for the hem.

4. Stitch three sides (sides and bottom), leaving the upper seam pinned.

5. Find an area where you can hang it — perhaps to a suitable curtain rod. Pin the three lengths of transparent green material to the top edge.

6. Now cut to a shape that suits your design. We used a loose scalloped line.

7. Each edge should be overlocked to prevent edge fraying. This stitching also prevents the material from hanging dead straight along the face of the altar.

8. Once you have overlocked the edges, stitch the layers to the top edge.

9. The material to cover the top surface of the altar is then cut to size, leaving an appropriate seam allowance.

10. Make up in the usual way and join to the frontal.

11. Feed the dowel through the seam. This added weight prevents the cloth from sliding forward and spoiling the finished look.

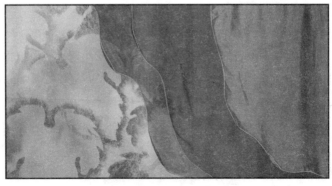

Detail of altar frontal

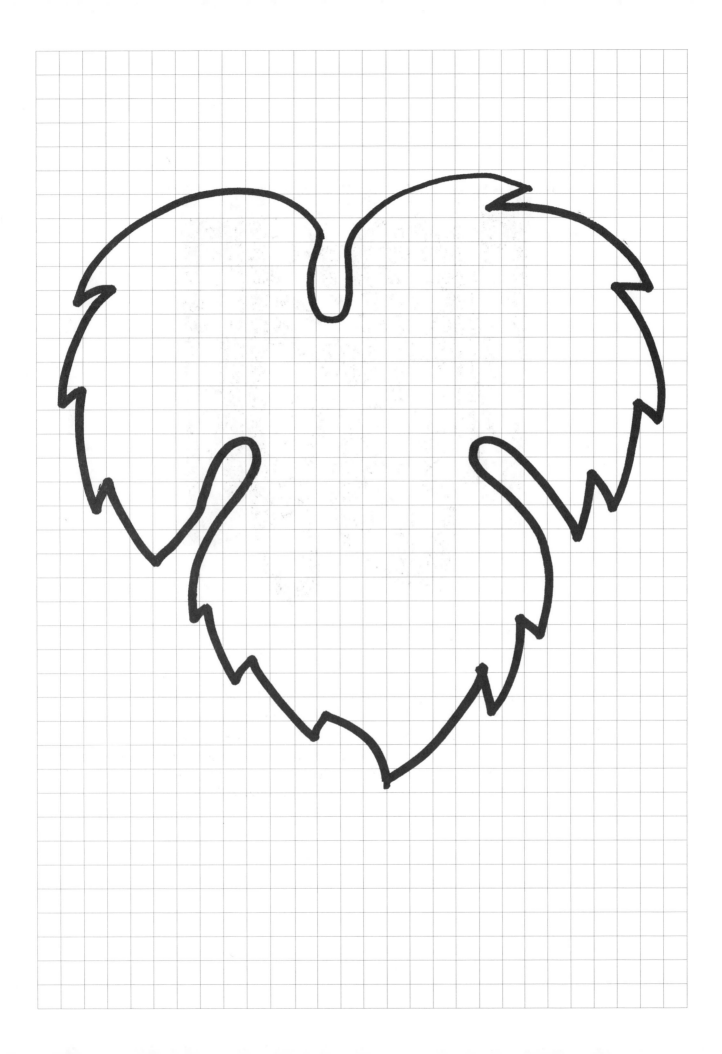

"The Lord Jesus on the night he was betrayed, took bread, and when he
had given thanks, he broke it and said, 'This is my body, which is broken
for you, do this in remembrance of me.' In the same way, after supper he took
the cup saying, 'This is the new covenant in my blood; do this whenever you drink
it, in remembrance of me.' For whenever you eat this bread and drink this cup,
you proclaim the Lord's death until he comes."
—I Corinthians 11:23-26

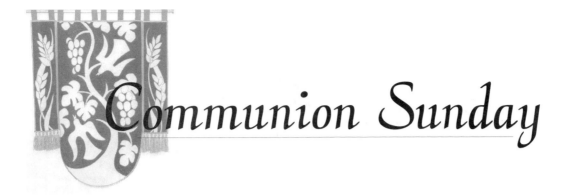

Communion Sunday

The inspiration for this banner comes from ancient classical times when the motif — birds (the faithful) feeding on the vine (the blood of Christ) — was often inscribed on sarcophagi. Heads of wheat symbolize the Bread of Life (Mark 14:22). Combining these symbols seemed a wonderful way of inviting people to participate in the Eucharistic Feast — the sacrament of Holy Communion.

The materials used are symbolic of wine and wheat: a rich burgundy velvet for the wine, and a plain muslin representing the more earthly wheat. Red braid was added to depict the blood, and the gold ribbon and finishing touches to remind us of God's glory.

The banner is approximately 64 inches x 75 inches. This does not include hanging loops at the top. The gold tassels hanging from the side panels are 8 inches in length and are made from gold crochet cotton. We've found that making our own tassels is far more cost-effective and they are equal in quality to the commercially made ones.

Sufficient fabric can be judged and measured once you have drawn up a full-sized template from the graph pattern. Feel free to increase or decrease the size, depending on its ultimate destination. The original graph size used was a 10-inch square.

The hanging loops are made from red corded material. Gold or burgundy loops would look just as good. If using gold material, I suggest you spray the dowel burgundy for a dramatic effect.

The banner is hung on a wooden curtain dowel that has been sprayed gold using a can of metallic spray paint.

The red cord used to outline the design can be purchased or can be easily made using red crochet cotton made into a daisy chain.

Required Materials

✓ Burgundy velvet or other suitable material

✓ Muslin for background material

✓ Muslin for backing

✓ Iron-on interfacing to cover design twice

✓ 30 yards of red cord (or make your own using crochet cotton)

✓ 6 yards of red braid and thin gold ribbon

✓ Gold crochet cotton for tassels

✓ 1 yard red fabric for hanging loops

✓ Wooden curtain dowel

✓ Spray paint

✓ Glue gun, fabric glue and the usual sewing aids

Detail of Eucharist banner

Instructions

To facilitate ease of handling, we constructed the banner in three separate pieces. Once fully completed, they were slip-stitched together.

1. Lay a sheet of interfacing on the full-sized template and trace the design motifs with a felt pen (a different color to the velvet). Side panels would be treated as separate pieces. One panel would be drawn on the wrong side of the interfacing to reverse the image.
2. The velvet is cut to banner size, allowing a 1-inch seam all around.
3. Carefully iron the interfacing onto the back of the velvet.
4. Cut the design motifs out of the velvet using sharp scissors.
5. Cut the muslin to the same size as the velvet and iron a layer of interfacing onto the back.
6. Gently place the velvet (right side up) onto the muslin and ease the design into the shape. Once you are satisfied it corresponds to the template design, glue down using fabric glue.
7. The next step is to secure the thin red braid or cord around the cut-out motifs. Use your glue gun for this task.
8. Velvet tends to shed fibers. Use a hair dryer on its cool setting to clear them away.
9. After creating all three panels, cut and trim the three pieces of your banner to the correct size.
10. Outline the pieces, using $^3/_4$-inch red braid, and glue down, using the glue gun. Once in place, glue down the gold ribbon that runs along the center of the braid.
11. Finally, finish the banner off by attaching backing cloth. Place the banner pieces onto the cloth and cut to size, leaving a 1-inch seam all around. Tuck the seam in and slip stitch the layers together. Before stitching, place the hanging loops between the backing and muslin layers in the correct sequence.
12. Sew the side panels onto the main body of your banner. Stitch the tassels onto the side panels.
13. Hang your banner on the dowel and enjoy your completed work!

"For this reason a man will leave his father and mother and be
united to his wife, and they will become one flesh."
— Genesis 2:24

Wedding

This banner is purposely kept small in size and unobtrusive in color. It only measures 24 inches by 48 inches. Candlewick stitching is worked on muslin in keeping with the traditions held dear at a wedding feast. It is designed to hang from a rostrum or pulpit or other appropriate spot. Change the design by appliquéing in vivid colors if so desired. Anything is possible. The design source is the chi-rho, XP being a monogram for Christ. The wedding rings are interlinked, with the X and P symbolizing Christ being central to our wedding vows. The wedding couple is represented by the stylized lily designs in the background.

Different colored threads and stitch patterns are used to add interest. Ribbon and ribbon roses add a soft touch, and a fine white and gold braid completes the finished banner. Brass rods and knobs are used at both ends for hanging.

When storing this banner, keep it well covered. Being light in color, it tends to soil easily. Lightly brush down after each use.

Required Materials

✓ ½ yard muslin for backing (just larger than your template)

✓ ½ yard white butter muslin (for candlewicking)

✓ ½ yard quilt batting

✓ Ribbon (cream and dark cream to blend with the muslin)

✓ Crochet number 5 cotton in blue and cream

✓ Gold metallic thread for the wedding rings

✓ Brass rod and knobs of your choice

✓ Gold and white braid to finish off the banner

✓ Glue gun, fabric glue and the usual sewing aids

Instructions

1. For accurate material requirements, use your template. Once you have completed your template, go over your design with a black felt-tipped pen. Place the muslin over the design and lightly trace. The design should be visible through the muslin.

2. Place the traced muslin over the batting and then onto the back piece of muslin.

3. Now proceed to candlewick, using different colored threads and stitches. French knots in gold are used for rings, and blue for the chi-rho. Cream is used for the lily designs. Border the design in lazy daisy and straight stitch in blue crochet cotton.

4. Ribbon is glued on using fabric glue. Ribbon roses are also glued into position at the corners of the ribbon borders.

5. Cut backing to size, leaving ½-inch seam. Tuck seam in and glue down.

6. Place your completed banner onto the backing and tuck in edges and pin. Using glue gun, glue backing to the banner.

7. Leave an opening at the top and bottom of the banner to slide dowels through for hanging.

8. Finally, glue gold and white braid to the edge.

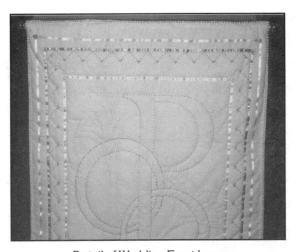

Detail of Wedding Feast banner

From Our Files

On the pages that follow you will find photographs of some of the banners that we have made over the years. Some have been made to hang in churches, halls, and even offices, while others have been made for special celebrations and worship services.

Our purpose has always been to glorify God through this particular art form, to enhance buildings and worship celebrations and to create banners through which God may communicate to his people.

We trust that the banners will not only give you pleasure, but also encourage you to seek inspiration from God and then to transform what he gives you into something beautiful for him.

Worship in Rural Africa

Promises of God

Jesus, King of Kings

Jesus, Lamb of God

Jesus, Lion of Judah

Such Love Banner

Renew Banner

Cross Banner

Power, Worship, Guide Banners

Truth, Praise, Witness Banners

About
Joyce Pike

Joyce was born in the small New Zealand town of Te Aroha and grew up in a family where knitting, sewing and handcrafts were part of life.

In 1968 Joyce emigrated to South Africa, along with her South African husband and their three young children. Two more children were born within the next few years. After being widowed for the second time, she married Eric Pike, a priest in the Anglican church. Only after their combined family of seven children had grown up was there time to depart from the basic skills of sewing to explore the art of appliqué, from which her banner ministry has developed and grown.

Frequently God gives the complete banner and appropriate Scripture to Joyce through dreams. With no training in design, putting these ideas on paper proved quite difficult. Joyce has enjoyed Anne's skill in this area, along with the way she has interpreted the ideas God has given her. Joyce and Anne have worked together on banners for several years.

About
Anne Robinson

Anne Robinson was born in Molteno, South Africa, in 1948. Her father was a medical doctor and her mother came from a farming community. She grew up in the Free State and completed her schooling in East London, where she presently resides and from where she works. She completed a diploma in fine arts in Durban. She also attended art college in St. Ives Cornwall, England.

Joyce Pike and Anne met about ten years ago when Eric, Joyce's husband, was resident pastor at St. Alban's Church, where Anne was a member. It was during this period that Anne started making banners, encouraged and influenced by the Pikes.

She believes that God has given her a special talent and she loves nothing more than using it to his praise and glory. She marvels at the way God has used her. It gives her great joy to be part of the banner-making ministry.

Order Form

Meriwether Publishing Ltd.
PO Box 7710
Colorado Springs CO 80933-7710
Phone: 800-937-5297   Fax: 719-594-9916
Website: www.meriwether.com

Please send me the following books:

_____ **Banners for All Seasons #BK-B250**   **$15.95**
by Joyce Pike and Anne Robinson
How to make creative banners for holy days and holidays

_____ **The Complete Banner Handbook #BK-B172**   **$14.95**
by Janet Litherland
A complete guide to banner design and construction

_____ **The Clown Ministry Handbook #BK-B163**   **$12.95**
by Janet Litherland
The first and most complete text on the art of clown ministry

_____ **Storytelling from the Bible #BK-B145**   **$12.95**
by Janet Litherland
The art of biblical storytelling

_____ **Worship Sketches 2 Perform #BK-B242**   **$15.95**
by Steven James
A collection of scripts for two actors

_____ **Service with a Smile #BK-B225**   **$14.95**
by Daniel Wray
52 humorous sketches for Sunday worship

_____ **Sermons Alive! #BK-B132**   **$14.95**
by Paul Neale Lessard
52 dramatic sketches for worship services

These and other fine Meriwether Publishing books are available at your local bookstore or direct from the publisher. Prices subject to change without notice. Check our website or call for current prices.

Name: _____ e-mail: _____

Organization name: _____

Address: _____

City: _____ State: _____

Zip: _____ Phone: _____

❑ **Check enclosed**
❑ **Visa / MasterCard / Discover #** _____

Signature: _____ Expiration date: _____
        (required for credit card orders)

Colorado residents: Please add 3% sales tax.
Shipping: Include $3.95 for the first book and 75¢ for each additional book ordered.

❑ *Please send me a copy of your complete catalog of books and plays.*